AF488405

Feel Your Heart And Light

Introducing
The Myofascial Release Approach
To Your Baby, Newborn Or Child

Feel Your Heart And Light: Introducing The Myofascial Release Approach To Your Baby, Newborn Or Child

ISBN: 979-8-9877496-0-9

First printing edition, 2023.

GroundswellMFR.com

Dedicated To

My child and warrior self,
You have been, are, and will always be, enough...

I love me.

Gratitude For

Teresa, Noah, Maximillian, Maddie, Chip and John F. Barnes

I love you.

Foreward

Dear teller of this tale,

Once upon a time, in a galaxy very nearby, and on a land very close to home, there lived a human being in a village who shared knowledge, wisdom, awareness, presence, power and love through a story, that connected in a story, that created a story, that became a story, without a story. And, as everyone in this village held this space, everything began to soften, healing and love emerged.

John F. Barnes, PT, is an international lecturer, author and authority on Myofascial Release. He is considered to be a visionary and teacher of the highest caliber. He has had the opportunity of training over 100,000 healthcare professionals in his Myofascial Release Approach. His goal is to help the therapist improve their logical\intuitive abilities, and confidence, thereby resulting in consistent and profound results for their patients. The John F. Barnes' Myofascial Release Approach® is considered to be the ultimate mind/body therapy that is safe, gentle and consistently effective in producing results that last.

In an excerpt from the preface of **Healing Ancient Wounds: The Renegade's Wisdom**©, John F. Barnes shares (and I offer that you consider doing the same with this book), "I suggest that this book be read differently than other books. Allow yourself to experience it visually, and with a felt sense. Be there in the moment! Consider stopping at each title, concept, or picture, slowing your breathing, softening your body, and quieting your mind. Think of the concept, and then quietly, without analysis, visualize whatever picture arises and feel whatever emotion emerges.

Then ask that picture and emotion to teach you. What does the visual/felt sense mean or symbolize to you? Allow this book to be a profound journey that will take you to a new depth of understanding, wisdom, and therapeutic effectiveness. The inner journey is not just the most important journey, it is the only journey! Let us now travel together, as I weave this tapestry, allowing us to connect with our 'essence,' that state of 'being' that brings quality and healing into our lives."

Perhaps sharing the space in which this story is about to be told offers an opening, or an opportunity for deepening the feeling of terminology, images and symbols connected through treatment following John F. Barnes' Myofascial Release Approach®. Its meaning, and its understanding are already within you, and resonate with those that guide you inward. So, as it is read, as the reader, allow for the creation of "space" that presents itself as the pause found in between the words that are read and spoken, in the turning of a page, or in between the beginning and the end. Give yourself permission to feel these moments, to observe, to appreciate, and to just be.

Whether you are reading this book for yourself or for another, please give yourself permission to do so without the pressure of having to explain or make sense of it to your listener, or to yourself. Simply by creating, and holding the space, allowing yourself, as the reader, to share its story, its message will arrive in whatever shape or form is needed, as it is needed, and wherever it is needed. If your listener or your mind's voice persists in their request for explanation, perhaps a response such as "Well, what does it mean to you?" or "What does that feel like to you?" may provide a starting, and continuing point inward.

Until next time...may all Be
with Love,
jeff

See John.

John

See John’s fascia.

(It connects him to everything)

John

See John's light.

John

Feel John's gentle hands.

Feel John’s light.

Can you slow your breaths going in?

Can you slow your breaths going out?

How does that make you feel?

me
mo

Can you soften your body
and become like ice cream
or marshmallow?

Where can you let go, and
soften
even more?

me
me
me

Feel your hands.

(Soften)

John
me

Feel your heart.

(Soften)

John

Feel your fascia.

(Soften)

John
me

Feel your light.

(Brighten)

John
me

Feel love
in
your heart.

John
me

Feel presence
in
your light.

John
me

Feel your heart
and light.

(It is everything)

I Love Me. I Love You.

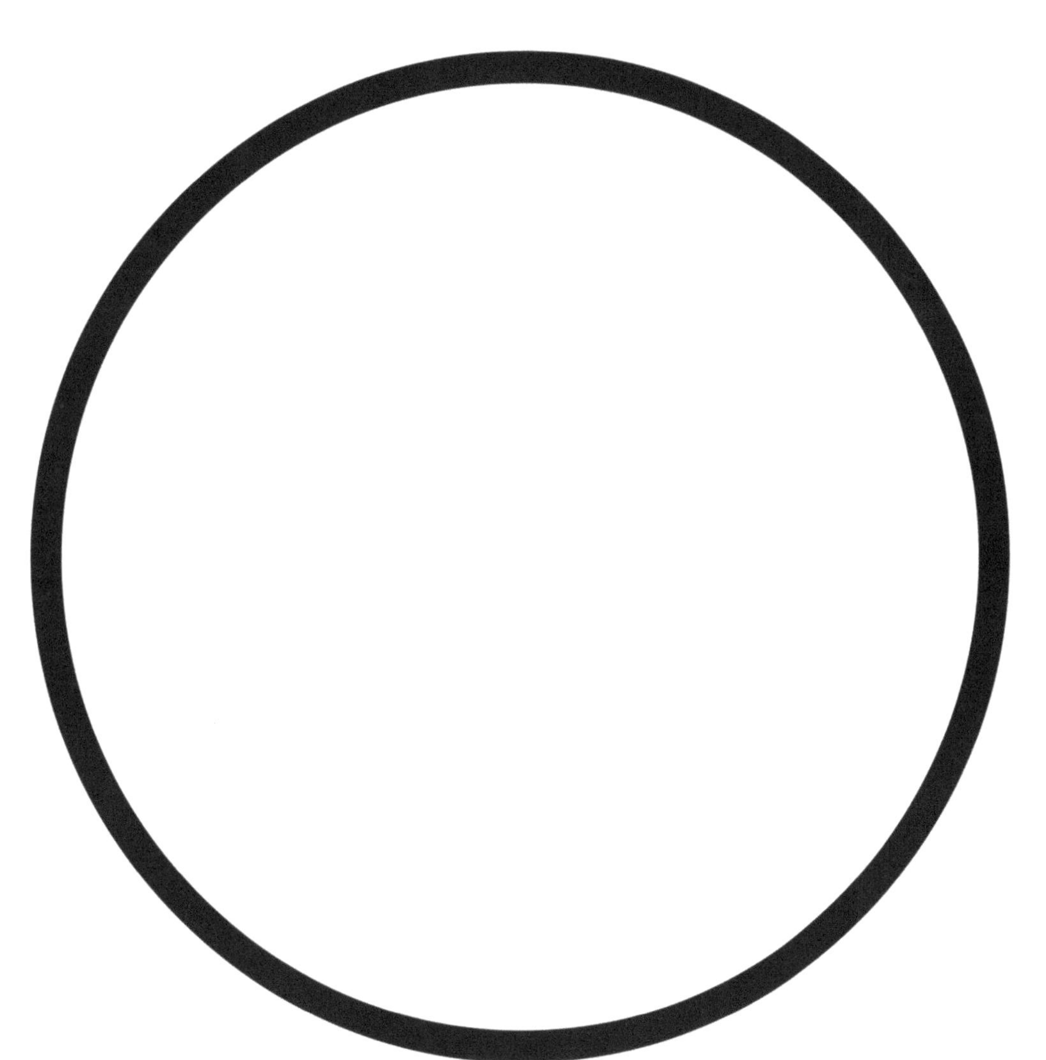

Afterward

During my treatment of the beautiful luminous essence from a six day old baby girl, I held the space to deliver a gentle and loving pressure at the site of a fascial restriction. All of this led to the sharing of a moment of presence, that expressed itself through a single tear emerging from her eyes. Eyes that were now wide open and revealed such a depth to me, of which I have never known. A message returned and resonated from my training and while receiving treatment for myself, the words offered by John, “If your tears could speak, what would they say?” In our connection, I felt them say, “thank you.”

Feel Your Heart And Light: Introducing The Myofascial Release Approach To Your Baby, Newborn Or Child begins a series of upcoming stories. Just as a drop in the ocean, begins a ripple, expands outward from its center, influences and connects with everything with which it meets; this story is being told so that mine, yours and ours may continue.

Thank you for Being.